Let God be God

Let God be God

HASKELL MILLER

Sermons for the
Sundays After Pentecost
(Sundays in Ordinary Time)
LAST THIRD
CYCLE C FIRST LESSON TEXTS FROM THE COMMON LECTIONARY

C.S.S. Publishing Co., Inc.
Lima, Ohio

LET GOD BE GOD

Copyright © 1988 by
The C.S.S. Publishing Company, Inc.
Lima, Ohio

All rights reserved. No part of this publication may be reproduced, stored in a retrieval system, or transmitted in any form or by any means, electronic, mechanical, photocopying, recording, or otherwise, without the prior permission of the publisher. Inquiries should be addressed to: The C.S.S. Publishing Company, Inc., 628 South Main Street, Lima, Ohio 45804.

Library of Congress Cataloging-in-Publication Data

Miller, Haskell M., 1910-
  Let God be God.

  1. Church year sermons. 2. Sermons, American. I. Title.
BV4253.M533   1988   252'.6   88-4345
ISBN 1-55673-062-4

8859 / ISBN 1-55673-062-4   PRINTED IN U.S.A.

Table of Contents

A Note Concerning Lectionaries and Calendars		7
Editor's Preface		8
Proper 21[1] Pentecost 19[2] Ordinary Time 26[3]	*Dead or Alive?* Joel 2:23-30	9
Proper 22 Pentecost 20 Ordinary Time 27	*Formula for Life* Amos 5:6-7, 10-15	17
Proper 23 Pentecost 21 Ordinary Time 28	*Of Preachers and Preaching* Micah 1:2; 2:1-10	25
Proper 24 Pentecost 22 Ordinary Time 29	*Counsel for Discouraged Disciples* Habakkuk 1:1-3; 2:1-4	34
Proper 25 Pentecost 23 Ordinary Time 30	*Let God Be God* Zephaniah 3:1-9	42
All Saints' Sunday [1,2] Ordinary Time 31[3]	*Why Aspire to Sainthood?* Daniel 7:1-3, 15-18	50
Proper 27 Pentecost 25 Ordinary Time 32	*The Now-ness of Eternity* Zechariah 7:1-10	58
Proper 28 Pentecost 26 Ordinary Time 33	*Life in the Sunbelt* Malachi 4:1-6	64
Christ the King	*The Reins of Power* 2 Samuel 5:1-5	72

[1]Common Lectionary
[2]Lutheran Lectionary
[3]Roman Catholic Lectionary

All texts in this book are from the series for Lesson One, Common Lectionary. Lutheran and Roman Catholic designations indicate days comparable to Sundays on which Common Lectionary Propers are used.

A Note Concerning Lectionaries and Calendars

The following index will aid the user of this book in matching the right Sunday with the appropriate text during the second half of the church year. Days listed here include only those appropriate to the contents of this book.

Fixed-date Lectionaries

Common	Roman Catholic	Lutheran Lectionary
Proper 21 *September 25 — October 1*	Ordinary Time 26	Pentecost 19
Proper 22 *October 2-8*	Ordinary Time 27	Pentecost 20
Proper 23 *October 9-15*	Ordinary Time 28	Pentecost 21
Proper 24 *October 16-22*	Ordinary Time 29	Pentecost 22
Proper 25 *October 23-29*	Ordinary Time 30	Pentecost 23
All Saints' Sunday *October 30 — November 5*	Ordinary Time 31	All Saints' Sunday
Proper 27 *November 6-12*	Ordinary Time 32	Pentecost 25
Proper 28 *November 13-19*	Ordinary Time 33	Pentecost 26
Christ the King	Christ the King	Christ the King

Editor's Preface

There is no correlation, in the Common Lectionary texts for the second half of the church year ("Sunday after Pentecost), between the First Lesson and the Gospel. The two sets of readings follow their own patterns. It is not likely, therefore, that the preacher using one set of texts would make any deliberate reference to the other.

Haskell Miller has, however, endeavored to find a connection wherever and whenever possible, between the First Lesson and the Gospel texts in each of the messages in this book. He has so intimately related the one to the other that we have included in the headings for each Sunday both the First Lesson and the Gospel texts. While we did not instruct Dr. Miller to bring about this marriage of texts, we think the result is a bonus for you.

Take and use. And let God be God as you proclaim him to your people.

Michael L. Sherer

Joel 2:23-30
Luke 16:19-31

Proper 21 (C)
Pentecost 19 (L)
Ordinary Time 26 (RC)

Dead or Alive?

What red-blooded member of the Western story and Western movie cult has not developed a fascination for the old-style posters proclaiming that someone is wanted "Dead or Alive"?

The Scriptures for today suggest we should have before us a series of posters with our pictures on them, each proclaiming in the boldest of print: "WANTED! Alive; not Dead!" This is the impression one gets from the whole biblical message.

Moses in his farewell address reminded the people that God had set before them blessing and cursing, life and death, and he pleaded with them to choose life. John reported that God's concern in sending Jesus into the world was that all who would respond in faith might have everlasting life.

Jesus wanted to help everyone have life — and have it in joyful abundance. In his great parable of the prodigal son, he ascribed the father's joy to the fact that a son who had been dead was now alive again. On one occasion, too, when Jesus was urging persons to follow him in meaningful living, he met the excuse of a funeral to attend by exclaiming, "Let the dead bury their dead!"

Obviously, in biblical parlance, as these references indicate, life and death have a spiritual as well as a physical dimension. This is the frame of reference within which the Scriptures read today must be interpreted.

"Look at the evidence of God's goodness, the blessings which he has bestowed upon you," Joel seems to be saying to the sons of Zion. "Wake up and live! Rejoice in the Lord, knowing that he is with you and is your God." When they become truly alive to God, the prophet goes on to affirm, their heightened sensitivity will enable both young and old to live beyond the limitations of time, space, and drab reality. They will dream dreams and have visions that make their lives transcendant.

In Luke's record of Jesus' parable about the rich man and Lazarus, the central theme seems to be that of life and death — principally death, in contrast to what life ought to be. In the dining room scene the tragic figure is not the poor, hungry beggar with dogs licking his sores. It is the indifferent rich man, who indulges himself in callous disdain of the other's need. He is dead, but does not know it. The intervention of physical death is only an incidental part of the story. After a reminder that eternity closes the door on time where the opportunity to live is involved, the scene shifts. The rich man's five dead brothers are brought into focus. Though they are still on the sunny side of physical death, they are so dead spiritually that no stimulus is capable of arousing a response in them.

What a dramatic story this is! Do we really get the point when we read it? From reactions I have encountered when trying to discuss the plight of the poor in our society, I can imagine a far too typical American reaction.

"What was wrong with the rich man enjoying his wealth?" I can hear someone ask. "He let the beggar have the crumbs, didn't he? And how come Lazarus was in that neighborhood, anyway? Didn't they have any vagrancy laws, or guards at the gate? And why had Lazarus become a beggar? Had he gotten into this condition because he was an irresponsible spendthrift, an alcoholic, or just a lazy bum?"

Is it possible that this kind of spirit has captured our moral sensitivities? If so, what do these evasive perspectives tell us about ourselves?

Clearly, Jesus' point in the story is that God wants dead people to come alive. How unfortunate it is, though, that we have so often viewed this concern as being focused primarily on physical resurrection after physical death. While there is needed comfort for us on this point, the main thrust of the Gospel is unquestionably toward bringing us to life spiritually before physical death forecloses the opportunity.

One cannot understand the Gospel without recognizing that it treats life and death as two-dimensional. In each it identifies both a material and a spiritual reality. Individual existence embraces both realities, but in a sharply contrasting developmental sequence. Physical existence proceeds from birth through life to death. Spiritual existence develops from death through birth to life. The function of physical life, one may conclude, is to serve as a launching pad, or birthing place, for spiritual life.

Since we are best acquainted with the processes in our physical development, let's concentrate for the moment on the realities involved in our spiritual development. We are spiritual as well as physical beings, and it is the spiritual side of our nature that tends to be most neglected.

What is the death out of which God wants to see a new birth occur?

A favorite sermon by a beloved pastor of the preceding generation was entitled "When a Man Is a Man." The text was from the Genesis account of Adam's creation. Not until some time after Adam had been formed did God breathe into him the breath of life. Then it was that he became a "living soul." There is a difference, declared this pastor, between an animate human body and one with a living soul. There are a lot of two-legged members of the *homo sapiens* species, he said, that are just walking possibilities. Not until the breath of God gets in them and they become living souls are they really men, or truly human.

Many of us have heard Saint Petersburg, Florida, referred to as the "City of the Walking Dead." The reason, of course, is that there are so many old people in it. The kind of deadness to which we are referring this morning, however, has nothing to do with physical aging.

How should it be explained? Can you think of illustrations? Have you ever seen anything like the deadness of the rich man who ignored poor Lazarus?

We are indebted to Sigmund Freud for a helpful frame of reference. He spoke, if you recall, of the "Id," "Ego," and "Super Ego" as being three levels of personal development and functioning. The "Id," he said, is the fundamental animal level, expressing the basic needs and drives of the physical being. The "Ego" is the level of self-conscious personhood. The "Super Ego" is the level of conscience and valuing. As a pathologist, Freud was concerned primarily with what happens to the person when unresolved conflicts develop between the "Super Ego" and the drives of the "Id" and "Ego." He did not throw much light, however, on what happens when the "Super Ego" fails to develop or take charge of the animalism of the "Id" and "Ego."

This, surely, is one of the points at which deadness of the spirit can be identified. How else should one describe a condition where there is an absence of compassionate sensitivity and responsibility for values?

Have you ever slept too long on a hard floor and had a limb "go to sleep" because circulation of the blood had been hampered? If so, the numbness has given you a hint of what physical death is like. Apply a tourniquet too long and real death of the appendage will occur.

I think of this often when I see persons who seem to have consciences that are asleep or dead. I wonder if they only need to be aroused to a life-giving flow of sensitivity, or if some unremoved tourniquet has produced irreversible death.

No doubt you have seen the television show entitled *Life Styles of the Rich and Famous.* Have you wondered, as I have, about these persons? How can they so freely immerse themselves in such opulence and self-indulgence in the presence, and often on the backs, of countless other persons suffering great need and deprivation? What has happened to their consciences? By what kind of twisted logic can they excuse themselves? And we may add, what does our envy of them say about us?

Something about such persons reminds me of the story of the Texan who, after a lifetime of frustrated striving, finally hit it rich in oil. The first thing he did was go to Dallas and buy himself his dream outfit — boots, spurs, a ten-gallon hat, all the trimmings, and a big Cadillac. No sooner had he arrived home, however, than he had a heart attack and died. His wife, conscious of his new-found pride and joy, decided that the only appropriate thing to do was to bury him with his new finery. Accordingly, a huge concrete vault was prepared in the cemetery and a large crane put in place. With his hat, boots, and new togs on, the body was placed at the wheel of the Cadillac. As the crane lifted the machine and began lowering it into the vault, one of the man's buddies nudged another standing close by and said, "Man, that's living!"

That, I fear, is like the living that is turning us into a society of alienated strangers, exploiting one another, forgetting God, and avoiding social responsibility. It is the mockery of life that makes us create cesspools of social neglect, and then brutalize the crippled persons who come out of them to disturb our peace. It is what makes us such fanatical racists, classists, religionists, or nationalists that we forget we belong, under God, to the whole human family. It is what makes us scorn poor and unsuccessful people with such arrangements as a welfare system that humiliates and punishes them.

The quality of life revealed in a society's functioning is indicative of how dead or alive spiritually are the persons of whom the society is composed. Considering the value distortions and alienation we have allowed to permeate our society and produce so many problems and inequities, it is not surprising that two authors were prompted to publish a book a few years ago under the title *God Is Dead*. Chances are, of course, that God is still in pretty good health. A more appropriate title for the book would have been *We Are Dead to God*.

The good news of the Gospel, however, is that death can be turned into life: physical death by means of the Resurrection; spiritual death by means of what Jesus spoke of as being born again.

What does it mean to be born again in this spiritual sense? If I had the wisdom to understand it fully, I would not have the words to explain it. One thing about it is clear, however. It means coming alive to God, opening the door to him, responding to his love, receiving his grace. It's a miracle of God's grace in which the endowment of our freedom gives us a significant volitional role.

Anthropologist James Breasted wrote a book some years ago entitled *The Dawn of Conscience*. Using the evolutionary perspective, he celebrated that early, unknown ancestor who first went beyond being merely an animal, and began seeking meanings, defining values, and trying to shape behavior by the results. Then it was, according to Breasted, that *homo sapiens* began to be human.

Truly, the formation and development of conscience is like a birth process. Conscience standing alone, however, is not enough. It needs direction and a point of reference in its functioning. Prompting and guidance by such a revelation as that which was in Jesus is essential. Only when conscience aspires to the highest and meets God in the network of response is it fulfilling its potential.

Who will not agree that a deadened conscience is the purest form of death this side of the grave?

A remarkable Tennessee storyteller gives an account of a barefoot mountain woman and her almost-grown barefoot daughter. They happened to have come into town when a big fire broke out on the main street. Fascinated by all the excitement and fire-fighting activity, they pushed up through the crowd as close to the fire as they could get. After a while, the girl said, "Ma, I smell flesh a-burnin." The mother looked down and around, and then replied, "Well, no wonder. You're standin on a live coal of far."

How many times have we seen people with deadened consciences, standing up close to tragedy or need, exhibit a similar level of insensitivity?

Jesus called us out of the shadows of sleep-walking death to wake up and live, to open our eyes in faith and let God bring fulfillment into our lives. When we hear and respond, it truly is like experiencing a new birth.

We may not describe our Christian experience in the same way as Charles Colson, a disgraced participant in the Watergate scandal. We can, however, understand the process by which he became a new and different man in Jesus Christ. His landing in prison shocked his conscience with awareness of the false values by which he had been living. Regretful awareness brought him to repentance, and faith reached out through Jesus in a cry for forgiveness and salvation. In the response of God's infinite and merciful love he became a new man.

It's an old, simple, tried-and-true formula that has worked again and again for countless persons through the ages.

But what is it like to be alive in Christ?

Saint Paul indicated that a maturation process is involved. Many stages of development are to be expected. Born again persons grow in grace. Babes in Christ move toward maturity and fullness of stature.

The common identifying characteristic is that of love trying to respond in obedience to the love of God. This leads toward the highest level of ethical sensitivity — a concern for what ought to be in terms of what is perceived to be the will of God. The purpose is to go with God's love wherever it goes in its outreaching embrace of the whole world. This concerned purpose at its beautiful best is marked by a redeemed imagination and a confident, courageous commitment.

We have seen these living features in the stories of the great saints of church history, in the lives of the missionaries who go out from our midst to selfless service in faraway places, and in the enthusiastic dedication of the young people who fill our theological seminaries. Let us not forget, either, the many pastors and lay persons whose unflinching faithfulness makes vital the life of the church. Such persons are marked, not by perfection but by a sensitive, persistent striving toward perfection. They undertake, in faith, to put aside inadequate values and relate themselves to what is highest and best. Depending on God's mercy and grace, they strive to follow Christ in the spirit of being God's children.

Jesus, I am convinced, was the most alive person who has ever lived. He was alive to and enjoyed a most intimate fellowship with God. At the same time, he was sensitively and compassionately alive to all the persons with whom he came in contact. He sensed and responded to people's needs, and even gave his life in love for all humanity.

I cannot forget a little book entitled *Human Destiny*, by a French writer named LeComte du Nouy. In it the author argues that all the processes of evolution have been pointed toward production of the kinds of persons that Jesus was.

I like to believe that this is the purpose in God's patient love — to lead the human family more and more into the life that was in Christ, to produce a maturity that will transcend sinful selfishness and the alienations and hatreds in which prejudice, social injustice, and war are rooted.

The bottom line for you and me in all this has to do with whether we are dead or alive. And if we are alive, whether we are striving toward greater maturity in Christ. Where do we fit in the picture of Lazarus, the rich man and his brothers, and the context of eternity? Are we, through the revelation in Jesus, choosing life and fulfillment? Or are we demonstrating a deadness that is frustrating the loving purposes of God for our lives?

What could be more appropriate for us than to be praying in such words as these from our hymn writers?

> *Breathe on me, Breath of God,*
> *Fill me with life anew,*
> *That I may love what thou dost love,*
> *And do what thou wouldst do.*
>
> *Open my eyes, that I may see*
> *Glimpses of truth thou hast for me;*
> *Place in my hands the wonderful key*
> *That shall unclasp and set me free.*

Amos 5:6-7, 10-15
Luke 17:5-10

Proper 22 (C)
Pentecost 20 (L)
Ordinary Time 27 (RC)

Formula for Life

A great old hymn asks, "And are we yet alive?" Last Sunday we saw in Luke's marvelous record of Jesus' teachings and in the prophetic injunction of Joel the contrast between life and death, and we were confronted with the challenge to live. Today as we continue with Jesus in Luke's record and hear the powerful voice of Amos speaking we discover the simple formula for living the life of faith.

For those who want life that is real, Amos says, there are two directions for their quest to take. They must seek fellowship with the Lord, and they must pursue good rather than evil.

Faith is important to life, Jesus indicates. It is infinitely powerful and enabling. But faith is its own reward. Do not expect special favors because you have it. To live in responsive obedience to God is to live by the formula for which life was intended. The meaning of life is in this fellowship, and that is reward enough.

Let us take a closer look at the basic elements in this life-formula as set forth by Amos and Jesus.

First and foremost is the emphasis on fellowship with God. We are reminded of God's special interest in us. We are his children. He loves us and has shared something of his own being with us. To live in alienation from him is to cut ourselves off from the source of our being. To know his love and be responding to it is to be warmed by the pulsebeat of life.

Is not this an important point for us — to pause and take

inventory of our personal life situations? How vigorously have we been consciously seeking a meaningful relationship with God? At what points, and by what practices, do we deliberately try to bring God and his will into the focus of our attention? Are we, for example, using, or have we discarded, such traditional practices as Bible reading, prayer, grace at mealtime, and regular attendance at public worship? Without these, have we found new and better, or more helpful, ways to seek and know God? Or is God simply relegated to the shadowy boundaries of our existence, to be called forth only when we get in a jam which we think we cannot handle by ourselves?

Let me hasten to add that I see no need for us to turn ourselves into overly pious ascetics in order to practice awareness of the presence of God. Fellowship with him should be an every-day, every-moment, commonplace, ongoing part of our normal experience.

The story of two little girls who were about to be late to a school presided over by a stern teacher comes to mind. One, in tears, said to the other, "Let's stop and pray that God won't let us be late." The other replied, "You can stop and pray if you want to, but I'm going to pray while I'm running."

How could the poet have been wrong when he said that prayer is "the soul's sincere desire, unuttered or expressed, the motion of a hidden fire that lingers in the breast"?

A prominent American philosopher, not noted for being particularly pious, has acknowledged that he makes it a habit each morning to engage in a simple but helpful practice which he considers prayer. He sits quietly for a period of about five minutes trying to identify the responsibilities of the day, and as he does so, without feeling the necessity of using words, he consciously puts himself in the mood of desiring that God direct his mind toward right perspectives on all the day may bring forth.

I have serious misgivings about persons who attribute their financial or other types of success to the fact that they have faith and have taken God into partnership with them. There are too many instances in the Bible where the faithful bemoan their misery in contrast to the prosperity of the unrighteous. I know that God does not always guarantee us success in our enterprises. To do so would be to deny us the freedom of responsibility and the opportunity for learning and growth. Nevertheless, the idea of partnership with him is a great one. This, I am sure, is what God wants. I have no doubt he always helps those whose lives are devoted to helping him.

The second important element in this formula for life is a natural accompaniment of the first. In almost the same breath that Amos says "seek the Lord and live" he adds "seek good and not evil, that you may live."

This simple injunction provides a clue to the fulfillment of life at the highest spiritual level. The essence of ethical, or truly godly and truly human, living is expressed in the quest for that which is good, which has most value in it.

The statement has been made that a person is living religiously when he is living up to the highest that he knows. I would like to revise it, however, to say that a person is living religiously when he (or she) is sincerely striving to live up to the highest that he (or she) knows, and when he (or she) is seeking always to know that which is higher.

If we are children of God the Creator, sharing in his creative nature, we are endowed with a capacity for creative striving, discernment, and valuing. To be unconcerned for the good and best is to go against the grain of purpose in our creation. It is to deny God in our lives, and to commit suicidal spiritual death.

What better explanation is there of what life is all about than that which is found in this simple truth? God has made us capable of valuing, of functioning creatively, as we experience the challenges of our existence. We are in fellowship with him, acting like his children, in harmony with the very ground of our being, when we are functioning as responsible valuers, aspiring to and choosing the good.

Shall we pause, in the light of this observation, to ask

ourselves a few probing questions? Are we alive to God in the realm of truth and values? Are we staying alert not only to what is good but also to the possibility of discovering what is higher and better? In other words, do we think we have arrived at all the truth we need to know? Or are we open and receptive to further revelations of truth and reality? It is important to be committed to the highest we know, but there is no stopping place in this commitment. Because the Creator God is still alive, and presumably still creating, our commitment must not become static, as though set in concrete. The Holy Spirit cannot continue its lifegiving work with a closed mind or a comatose conscience.

Jesus, in the lesson read from Luke, commends faith as an important dimension of power in the life that is alive to God. The energy in the atom is not to be compared with the power he sees can be released in the life of faith. His homely analogies are a mustard seed and a moving mountain.

Dare we inspect our faith? Is it safe for us to engage in such a diagnosis of our spiritual health?

Are we even clear as to what it is we are talking about when we speak of faith? The New Testament writer's statement that it is the "substance of things hoped for, the evidence of things not seen" is helpful but ambiguous. It emphasizes aspiration and confidence, but is very unspecific in orientation.

Too often we have cheapened our profession of faith into a perfunctory ritualistic exercise of giving verbal assent to a creedal statement of beliefs.

Another evidence of our great confusion on the subject is represented in the utilitarian notion that faith will enable us to get what we want. The business entrepeneur expects faith to help him get rich. The physically afflicted expect faith to help them get well. The persecuted expect faith to deliver them from their persecutors. Those who try to exercise faith through prayer expect it to work magic and produce the answers they desire.

Faith and its expression in prayer are not, however,

primarily utilitarian instruments. To be sure, they have a great bearing on our economic endeavors, our health, and every other aspect of our lives. They are effective means for relating ourselves to God, the source and ground of our being. But they are not tools to be used in trying to manipulate God.

I cannot forget the immature, pious, young fundamentalist preacher who made a point of exercising what he called his faith during the trying days of World War II. Gasoline was strictly rationed, and it was illegal for anyone to transfer gas coupons to anyone else. This young man, who was residing in Louisiana, decided, however, that he would make an automobile trip to Chicago. It was not an essential trip, and he did not have gas coupons for it. But upon being challenged about the gas problem, he said he had faith that the Lord would provide. Sure enough, he made the trip successfully. He did it by talking piously to people along the way about being a minister and needing additional coupons for his ministerial responsibilities. In this way he persuaded several persons to share their coupons with him. On his return, he declared his success was evidence of the power of faith. Persons who knew him and what he had done, however, found other ways of explaining the matter.

Jesus, in the Gospel taken as a whole, strongly intimates that faith is an empowering experience of *in-Godness*, an enthusiastic confidence in and closeness of fellowship with God. The assurance and confidence are rooted in the reality of the fellowship. They emanate from a living awareness of God's love, mercy, grace, and companionship.

In this context, faith means obedience to the will of God. It means not reluctant submission to an imposed will, but a glad union of wills formed in a fellowship of love. Responsive love in the person alive to God seeks to obey God's love by becoming one with it.

Are we, then, living the life of faith? Are we making our lives expressions of confident in-Godness? Is the salvation we seek that of God's kind of fulfillment in our lives? Or are we looking upon faith as a means to lesser ends — like getting what we want or getting to heaven when we die?

This brings us to the main thrust, in Jesus' words from the Scripture reading today. On the surface, it seems harsh and somewhat out of character for him to be asking his hearers to identify with a master who deals with his servant in rulebook fashion. Though the servant comes in tired from the plow, Jesus says, he is still required, according to the custom of the day, to prepare and serve the master's meal before expecting the privilege of seating and serving himself. The arrangement is not unusual, but a simple fulfillment of expected roles.

"So you also," Jesus concludes, "when you have done all that is commanded you, say, 'We are unworthy servants; we have only done what was our duty.' "

Let it be remembered, however, that Jesus' words about faith and its power immediately preceded this illustrative analogy. The analogy is not about the social arrangement of power relations between master and servant. It is about the servant's attitudes and expectations. What does he expect from his role of servanthood other than that he has filled it well? To live as one should, to have the satisfaction of knowing that one's duties have been fulfilled to the best of one's abilities, is all the reward that should be expected.

It is as though Jesus was saying, "What do you expect as rewards for your faith and good behavior? Are you looking for special favors beyond a simple commendation for being good and faithful servants?"

This comes awfully close to being a deserved rebuke to us for our unrealistic expectation of divine favors for obeying the rules and doing the good deeds of Christian living. Too often the spirit in our performance suggests that we are trying to accumulate brownie points toward special prizes, either in this world or the next.

What we should be aware of is that the rewards for righteousness do not come as medals or special bonuses. They are in the joy and fulfillment that inhere in right living. The saints who have lived out their faith and the martyrs who have died for it have demonstrated this truth again and again.

The delivery van driver who saw the horrible plane crash in the Potomac River in Washington, D.C., on that frigid day a few years ago was not cruising around looking for a chance to win awards for being a hero. He was just a sensitive, caring type of human being. His only thought when he saw a young woman struggling in the icy water was to try to save her. His jumping in and pulling her to safety was an expression of the kind of person he was. The satisfaction of knowing that he had done what he could was a greater reward than all the medals and accolades that could be heaped upon him. To have failed to respond with the strength he possessed would have been to deny meaning in his existence.

A professor in a course on character education made an impressive comparison between scouting and the 4-H Club program. Both, he said, are aimed at developing character in young people. Scouting, in his opinion, however, was less effective than the 4-H program. His reasoning was that scouting relied on artificially contrived activities for which badges and trivial rewards were offered. The 4-H programs, on the other hand, involved youth in real life activities with built-in compensations. No less important than the immediate returns were the development of skills and capacities directly related to lifetime activities.

Whether or not this is a fair appraisal of the two programs, the point made is quite relevant to our discussion. The Christian religion is not something to be artificially imposed on life. It is the essence of real living.

So what is the formula for real life as Amos and Jesus outline it for us? It is to seek the Lord, pursue good rather than evil, maintain faith-filled confidence in God, and appreciate the opportunity for fulfillment in living life attuned to the will and purpose of God. No magic; no fancy frills; no artificial inducements! Just faithful servants; loving children of a loving God.

If we underscore the word "live," we may discover a special meaning in Paul's words, so prized by Martin Luther, that "the just shall *live* by faith."

Micah 1:2; 2:1-10 Proper 23 (C)
Luke 17:11-19 Pentecost 21 (L)
Ordinary Time 28 (RC)

Of Preachers and Preaching

Of the several significant themes which may be identified in the Scripture lessons read today, I choose the one about preachers and preaching. Perhaps this is because I tune in most easily on this wave length.

The prophet Micah came out of the village of Moresheth with a message concerning Samaria and Jerusalem which he was sure the Lord wanted him to deliver. It was a social Gospel message condemning the prominent and powerful of those societies for their many sins. "Have you no sense of justice?" he shouted at "the heads of Jacob and rulers of the house of Israel." The Lord's charge against you, he declared, is that you "eat the flesh of my people, and flay their skin off them, and break their bones in pieces, and chop them up like meat in a kettle, like flesh in a caldron."

After detailing many of the abuses of power and privilege which gave rise to this denunciation, the prophet predicted that great humiliation and suffering would be brought upon the lands by such behavior. "Zion," he said, "shall be plowed as a field; Jerusalem shall become a heap of ruins." Nothing short of this could be the consequence of the social chaos which was being generated.

Not surprisingly, this sharp-edged message was not well received. Micah was not the most popular evangelist who ever came to town. Any courageous pastor of a modern prestige church on Main Street or in the suburbs could easily have predicted what the reaction would be. The record does not tell us all that transpired, but it does report that the preacher was sharply rebuked by being told that "one should not preach of such things." The power brokers, wheelers-and-dealers, and dowager ladies lost no time in informing him that he did not know what he was talking about; that no such calamity and disgrace as he predicted could ever take place.

Eventually, in frustration and disgust, Micah concluded that "if a man should go about and utter wind and lies saying, 'I will preach to you of wine and strong drink,' he would be the preacher for this people."

Doubtless one could find many preachers today with similar sentiments — preachers who have been rebuked or lost their pulpits for advocating needed social change, while other preachers, mouthing safe traditions and avoiding controversy, have prospered or even been lionized. Micah could have been looking down the corridors of time and seeing a long line of splendid windbags standing in pulpits and congratulating people on the comfortable lifestyles being enjoyed on foundations of evil social practices. He was convinced, however, that his ministry should be more than pious God-talk or providing comfort to the afflicted. He knew that God wanted him to help afflict the comfortable.

If Micah were teaching in one of our theological seminaries today, or speaking in one of our retreats for pastors, we can imagine the direction of his challenge. It is not at all likely that he would leave the impression that ministerial responsibility is adequately discharged in the stereotyped processes that have been described as "hatching, matching, patching, and dispatching."

An especially insightful and frustrated preacher of whom I know must have taken his cue from Micah. What the people of his congregation needed, he declared, was to be weaned from their baby food diet of sweet pap and made to chew on some tough beefsteak, or maybe even some distasteful shoe leather.

While we are thinking of Micah's experience, however, let

us look at that of Jesus as described in the Gospel for today. Jesus was not exactly preaching, but it is not stretching a point too much to see a similarity in the response of his audience and that of the audience to which Micah spoke.

Jesus told the ten lepers what to do in order to be cured of their affliction. They obeyed his instructions because their self-interest was involved. Only one however, had the sensitivity of spirit to respond with a show of gratitude.

Let us make note in the very beginning, therefore, that the spiritual condition of the audience can have a powerful influence on preachers and their preaching.

This is especially true in today's situation, where the audience usually controls the purse strings of the preacher's livelihood. Audience responses such as Micah and Jesus encountered can have a powerfully coercive influence on modern preaching.

Bear this in mind as we continue to pursue the subject of preachers and preaching.

Since the time of Micah and Jesus there have been many preachers — good, bad, and indifferent. A few have deserved to be called prophets. Some have been charlatans and frauds. The great majority, however, have been sincere individuals striving, within the limitations of their abilities and the receptivity of their listeners, to be faithful in delivering the comforting and challenging good news of God's love and redeeming grace.

But who are the preachers? What kind of strange creatures are they? And what qualifies them for their special role?

It did not take me long after entering the ministry to become sharply aware that I was considered somehow different from other people. This distressed me because I did not feel all that different, and I spent too much energy trying to shuck off the stereotypes people persisted in imposing upon me. Let me take this opportunity, therefore, to assure you of what you doubtless have discovered already — that preachers are very human human beings.

In most protestant circles the tradition has been that they

are men, like Micah, with a uniquely special calling from God. Are you aware of how that image is now being changed in several basic respects?

In the first place, the male monopoly of God's messenger service is being effectively challenged. It is being recognized that God may have something to say to and through women as well as men. Consequently, the voices of more and more women are being heard from the pulpits of the churches. The number of women enrolled in our theological seminaries is fast approaching parity with the enrollment of men.

Experience has taught the churches also to modify reliance on the individual's sense of a special mystical calling. A sense of calling is still considered imperative, of course, but it has seemed necessary for the nature and authenticity of the call to be scrutinized carefully by the community of faith. The church could not long survive if it gave equal and unqualified attention to all the eccentric individuals who get a feeling of being called.

The point is illustrated in an old story about a country boy who claimed to have a vision that propelled him into the ministry. According to his report, as he was at work in the fields one day he had looked up to see the capital letters G P C blazing across the sky. Filled with awe, he had interpreted these letters to mean "Go Preach Christ." After listening to him try to preach a few times, however, bearing witness to his vision, one of his aged, crusty neighbors said, "Son, them letters didn't mean 'Go Preach Christ,' they meant 'Go Plow Corn.' "

Another modifying influence on the subject of calling is the need for pastors of the many churches which have been established. This need is too great and too specialized to be left to the chance that solitary individuals functioning in the isolation of their solitude will be prompted in sufficient numbers to listen to God's call to fill these roles. It has been perceived as a responsibility of the church to help articulate God's call by nurturing in its midst awareness of the need for this type of ministry.

For many individuals these days, therefore, the G P C vision might appear as in neon lights over denominational headquarters. Respondents, moreover, would be dependent on an examining board of the church to help them determine whether the intended message was "Go Preach Christ" or "Go Plow Corn." In addition, when their calling has been thus authenticated, they may expect the requirement of a disciplined process of education and training before they are considered fully qualified for ministry.

The process should not be disparaged, nor should the individuals who are qualified through it. It is a rational way of "testing the spirits" and assuring the church of capable leadership. Only individuals with a special sense of purpose and dedication are likely to be selected and qualified through it.

That there are risks involved, however, in the procedure and the style of ministry to which it points must be recognized. A danger exists that the preacher will be seduced into becoming merely an organization person, forgetting, neglecting, or not having heard the cutting message of change and challenge which God wants delivered with reference to specific times, places, and conditions. The preacher-pastor so selected, moreover, may become so immersed in traditionalisms and so involved in the routine functions of church administration and pastoral care that the possibility of receiving and delivering special, first-hand messages from God becomes exceedingly remote.

Further complicating the situation is the fact of an ever-present possibility of not-so-subtle intimidation. The sincere preacher-pastor who tries to stay responsive to the living God and deliver messages of special relevance he or she believes God wants delivered will encounter much resistance. From the pew all the way up to denominational headquarters voices likely will be raised to say, "You should not preach of such things." Persistence may lead even to unemployment or loss of credentials.

The problem is not new. Micah recognized it when, as recorded in the third chapter of his message, he deplored the fact that "priests teach for hire" and "prophets divine for money." In other words, he was keenly aware of the fact that people who pay the bills tend to have a controlling influence on the message.

Need I remind you of the pastors who have been removed from their pulpits for speaking out about such matters as slavery, race relations, class snobbery, exploitation of labor, national policy, and involvement in war? Do you realize how risky it is at the present time for a pastor to go against the grain of public opinion on such matters as homosexuality, abortion, welfare policy, treatment of criminals, the merits of capitalism, or the ethics of nuclear deterrence?

Yes, preachers are supposed to be called of God. They are supposed to be in touch with the living God. They, like Micah, are supposed to deliver the word, not merely as it has been derived from past revelation but also as it has come to them directly from their experience with God. But there are many impediments in the way.

Quite understandably, some preachers find it safer, therefore, to stay strictly with what the Bible says than to seek any fresh, updated insight into God's continuing revelation of truth. People, they have found, seem more comfortable with the thought that God was alive and speaking in the past when the Bible was written than they are with the thought that he is still alive and interacting with his people today.

There is, of course, no pat formula for preaching. As the occasion requires, it may be teaching, exhorting, or simple witnessing.

A story about Saint Francis records that he once invited a young novice to go with him into a nearby village to preach. The young man gladly accepted the invitation, anxious to hear and assist with the great man's message. With Saint Francis in the lead they walked all the way through the village and back to the monastery without pausing to make a single speech. On arriving at the monastery gate, the young man protested, "But I thought we went to the village to preach!" "We did preach," Saint Francis replied. "There is no need to go anywhere to preach unless you preach everywhere you go."

Preaching also may and ought to be prophetic. This has nothing to do with mystical foretelling. It is rational forthtelling by persons who speak from two solidly established vantage points. One is that of a close relationship with God and careful attention to his revealed word. The other is that of a clear-eyed, informed appraisal of reality in the situation to which it is deemed that God wants his word addressed.

Prophetic preaching embraces the dimension of Christian ethical responsibility. It sets what ought to be, what God wants, over against what is. It challenges God's children to function as responsible valuers in the light of all revelation they have received.

As you can see, preaching is no small undertaking. Good preaching must inform, instruct, sensitize, challenge, convict, and seek commitment. It can never be flippant or casual. Though it is a joyous and privileged task, it is very serious business.

And now in case you are wondering why I say all this, let me assure you that it is not for the purpose of eliciting your sympathy for the complexities of the role I am trying to fill as your preacher and pastor — although sympathy is always comforting, of course, when a fellow can get it.

My real concern, however, is to try to be frank with you about how I perceive myself in my role as your pastor, and to have you join with me in the purpose of making our ministry together as meaningful as possible. To this end let me pose some pointedly personal questions, the answers to which could be as important to you as to me.

For example, what kind of preaching do you want to hear, or are you willing to listen to? Can I speak to you freely from my heart in the light of my fullest understanding of the word and will of God? Will you listen if I try to preach about your sin, God's judgment, and your need of repentance, as well as about the love, mercy, and grace of God? Is it safe for me to address your prejudices, challenge your greed, question your values, or point to deficiencies in your behavior?

What if I try to bring my understanding of the Word of God to bear on problems and issues in our community, nation, and world? Are you prepared to accept the fact that the Gospel is social as well as personal? Can you bear the pain of joining me in trying to stand apart with our Lord and take an objective look at our attitudes, habits, social patterns, institutions, and total culture? What will be your attitude if, with humility and sincerity, my interpretation cuts across the grain of your opinions?

God, I am persuaded, wants you and me to stay open to instruction by the Holy Spirit, to stay alive, alert, and growing. His goal, as Paul indicated, is to help us reach full maturity in Christ. His purpose in all preaching he directs to us, therefore, is to help us attain this objective — though, I hasten to add, he wants us to deal creatively, not submissively, with all that we hear.

So it will be well if you ask yourself today why you come to church and listen to a preacher. What do you want to hear? Is it your wish to be congratulated or to be challenged? To be confirmed in your opinions or shocked into new awareness? To be soothed and comforted or aroused to repentance and action? Can you be counted on for a more sensitive response than Micah found in his audience or than Jesus witnessed in the nine lepers?

And now to conclude all this let me remind myself and you that I have been speaking, for the most part, from within a limited, segmental view of the ministry. I have been talking about the specialized role of the professional who carries out certain duties assigned by the church. The New Testament makes it plain, however, that all of us who are sincere followers of Christ are ministers of his Gospel. We are all called, all witnesses, all missionaries.

The pulpit and pastoral ministry as the church has established it is only one of the channels through which our calling may be directed. The persons who function in this specialized professional role are engaged in what is properly called "the equipping ministry." Their job is to help all the faithful carry out their witnessing and evangelizing tasks.

So you are in the ministry as well as I. Isn't it unfortunate that we can't get our preaching better coordinated? Do you sense, as I do, a great need for us to move beyond our fragmented efforts to throw monologues at one another, to a more effective cooperative witness as the Body of Christ? Let's resolve to try to be more in dialogue with one another and more incorporate in Christ with our preaching. We need to be listening carefully to each other, as well as to the Lord, in order to be clearer about what the Spirit is saying to the churches and what the churches should be saying to the world.

Habakkuk 1:1-3; 2:1-4 Proper 24 (C)
Luke 18:1-8 Pentecost 22 (L)
Ordinary Time 29 (RC)

Counsel for Discouraged Disciples

John Bunyan had a remarkable ability to represent everyday truth in impressive allegory. One of the most vivid representations in his story, *Pilgrim's Progress,* has to do with what happened in the Valley of Humiliation.

No sooner had Pilgrim entered this valley than he saw the foul fiend Apollyon bearing down upon him, breathing fire and smoke. Pilgrim's first impulse was to turn and flee for his life. As he was about to do so, however, he remembered that the only armor he wore was on his front side. Reasoning quickly in the light of this fact, he decided that if he had nothing more in mind than simply trying to save his life it would be better to stand and face the evil dragon than to expose his unprotected rear to the firey darts.

This approximates the message in the Scripture lessons read this morning.

The prophet Habakkuk bemoans the fact that he has been forced to experience much trouble and look upon many terrible wrongs. He complains that he has cried to God for help and that his cries apparently have not been heard. He cannot see any way out of the tangled mess that engulfs him.

In the midst of his depression and protest, however, he gets a message which, put in the slang of our day, was, "Hang in there! Don't give up the ship!" Or, in the words of the scriptural record, the Lord said to him, "The vision awaits its time

... wait for it; it will surely come ... the righteous shall live by his faith."

Paraphrasing this, it seems to me the Lord is saying to the discouraged prophet, "Do not be impatient. There is a way out, and it will be made plain in time. Remember that faith is essential for a person who lives for what is right."

The selection read from Luke's record emphasizes the same theme. Jesus had been talking to his disciples about some of the trying experiences he was sure they soon would be encountering. Then he told them a parable which, according to Luke, was to the effect that they ought always to pray and not lose heart. The parable was about a widow who tried to get a thick-skinned judge to justify her in a complaint she had against someone who had done her wrong. For a long while the judge refused to do anything about her case. After she kept on and on, however, he finally decided to vindicate her to stop her from pestering him. If this kind of judge will yield to such persistence, Jesus asked, "Will not God vindicate his elect who cry to him day and night?"

Need we remark that there are enough terrible evils in today's world to discourage anyone? Many of the most sensitive souls among us are being victimized by destructively immobilizing depression. How many of us have totally escaped sensations of what is being called "nuclear numbness"? The more sensitive and aware persons are, the more they are at risk to this type of dreadful illness.

This comes sharply to focus for me when I think of the tragedies of suicide, alcoholism, and mental illness I have known. Almost universally the individuals involved have been among the most sensitive and beautiful spirits of my acquaintance. The only appropriate generalizing way I have found to describe them is to say that they were victims of unfortunate social circumstances.

There was, for example, the lovely young Sunday church school boy more than forty years ago who was snatched from his warm-hearted adoptive home and put in the army to be made a killer for World War II. Though he was not physically injured, he was effectively destroyed. Through all the years since he has been staring vacantly into unknowing nothingness within the walls of one of the institutions where we store our social discards.

There was the little twelve-year-old black girl who hanged herself in the closet of a shabby home in the inner city. Unloved, abused, exploited, she had had enough years to explore the depths of despair.

A disturbed Jewish university student also comes to mind. He had been unable to measure up academically to the expectations of unloving parents. He had been taunted and tormented throughout his childhood in a congested urban neighborhood where prejudice against Jews was strong, and had found himself too self-conscious and physically unattractive to achieve satisfying acceptance among his peers on the university campus. No wonder he had come to the point of being unable to function!

Finally, I must mention the quiet, attractive, black youth of the inner city who confided his guilt with shame. Because he had been unable to find employment and was part of an impoverished family he had made himself a criminal by committing a robbery in order that his younger brothers and sisters might have a few small presents for Christmas.

The list of such examples could be extended indefinitely. We live in a harsh and cruel world. Behind the massive statistics on suicide, mental illness, alcoholism, crime, delinquency, and the like, are warm-hearted human beings. We can label them sinners or weaklings, but do the labels conceal more than they reveal? My guess is that the individuals are indeed more fragile, but possibly also more sensitive and aware, than most of us.

Who can look upon the evils which surround us and not be affected? Who can be impervious, for example, to: the greed and hunger; the exploitation and poverty; the suffering and neglect; the oppression and denial of human rights; the cut-throat competition and callousness toward the unsuccessful; the crime and delinquency; the slaughter of innocents on our highways; the corruption of politics; the strangle hold of the military-industrial complex that feeds on society's paranoia; the awful apparition of nuclear weapons in the hands of posturing politicians threatening to use them; the monster of war attached like a leech to the underbelly of civilization; the racial prejudice and discrimination; the religious bigotry and intolerance?

These are but a few of the conditions that try human souls in our time. No wonder Bertrand Russell, even in pre-nuclear days, was prompted to say that "unyielding despair is the only legitimate state of mind for modern man!"

Christians, whose consciences have been made especially tender by the love of God perceived in Jesus Christ, cannot avoid being perturbed by such evil conditions as they daily encounter. After all, the Christian religion is an ethical religion. It prompts persons to look with critical evaluation at existing conditions, and beyond them to what ought to be, to what God wants.

But sincere Christians are not merely aware of things that are wrong. They hurt with a sensitivity drawn from the love of God revealed in Jesus. The sight of evil pains them; causes them suffering; makes them want to join Jesus in cross-bearing efforts to bring about redemptive change.

Regardless of the sincerity of their dedication, however, they are never emancipated from the pain and frustration in cross-bearing. Evil never surrenders without a fight. The wrongs that are resisted often seem to grow more monstrous the more they are opposed. Lifetimes of tears, prayers, and strenuous involvement may pass without seeming to make much difference.

The risk of discouragement, therefore, is always great. And discouragement unrelieved tends toward depression and despair.

Of all the sad sights to meet the eye, one of the saddest

is that of the bright-eyed, eager disciple who, like young Judas, upon encountering discouraging reality becomes disillusioned, abandons the vision, and glides toward the chasm of despair.

Church history is replete with examples of individuals who made a great start in the Christian life but failed. They found the struggle against evil too much for them. In particular, the number of those burned out after dabbling with Christian social action has been exceeded only by the number of those who have closed their eyes to social evil and sought salvation without personal involvement.

Jesus was greatly concerned both that evil be resisted and debilitating discouragement avoided. He challenged his disciples to take up their crosses and follow him. He instructed them to make concern for the coming of the Kingdom of God on earth the prayerful passion of their lives. He commissioned them to go into all the world with the good news of the Gospel.

At the same time, he prayed for them that they would be kept from, not overwhelmed by, the evil. Moreover, he obviously saw the evil as existing at both the personal and the social levels. It is fascinating to speculate on what he meant when he said "the kingdom of God is within you." Was he saying "it is inside you personally" or "it is in your midst as a group," or did he mean both? In any case, the implication is that if God is on the throne within you, there is nothing that can defeat you.

Much time in Jesus' brief ministry was spent in counseling the disciples against discouragement. The parable in today's Gospel lesson is only one among many examples. A few basic emphases in his counseling are easily identified, and they are just as important for us today as they were to the band of twelve to whom they were originally addressed.

Some of these emphases should have our special attention:

First, the emphasis on having and maintaining faith.

Believe in God and believe in me, he said. Without a settled conviction at the core of one's being, he knew that persistent faithfulness would not be possible. Doubtless, he knew the story of Job's saying of God "though he slay me, yet will I trust him." Certainly, he understood that with such a conviction, what Paul later described as "the substance of things hoped for, the evidence of things not seen" would be possible as reassuring reality, come what may.

Second, note his emphasis on keeping faith animated by love.

Love was all-important to Jesus. He made it clear that God is love, and encouraged his followers to immerse themselves in the ethos of love, loving God back and going with his love. Love one another and love your neighbor as yourself, he said. Then, by the use he made of the cross, he demonstrated that love rooted in faith couquers all.

Third, Jesus assumed that faith and love must find their expression in courage.

He did not hesitate to challenge his disciples to the fearsome tasks of cross-bearing. He warned them against the unworthiness of putting their hands to the plow and then turning back. And one of his greatest admonitions to them came at the conclusion of his passionate remarks following the last supper in the upper room. In the King James Version his words were, "Be of good cheer, I have overcome the world." I prefer the translation, however, that has him saying, "Courage! I have conquered the world."

He knew that faith and love must have in them a backbone of courage if they are to make a significant impact on the lost and sinful world.

Jesus' emphasis on prayer must also have special consideration.

Pray to your heavenly father, he said; pray without ceasing. Do not be discouraged if you seem not to be getting the answers you expect. To him prayer obviously was communion and fellowship with God. It was habitual and continuous, not occasional or whimsical. Prayer was what enabled him to testify that he was not alone because the Father was with him, and to speak with assurance of the fact that he was in the Father and the Father was in him.

Finally, we should note that Jesus counseled against the idea of trying to go it alone.
His emphasis on prayer was to this point. Because they were to be in partnership with God they would never be laboring alone. Not only would God be on their side; the Holy Spirit would be present with them for guidance and comfort.

What great and good counsel is found in these guidelines and emphases! Where is the therapist who could speak more directly and helpfully to our spiritual need?

How shall we, his latter-day disciples, respond to this counsel? Shall we assess the quality of our faith, the extent of our love, the depth of our concerns, the sincerity of our commitment, the degree of our courage, the validity of our prayer life? Shall we check up on ourselves to make sure we are involved with God in his agenda, rather than trying to go it alone in pursuit of our own personal agendas?

If we find ourselves among the masses of the spiritually neurotic and sick, will we try to listen to Jesus that we may become well, healthy, and strong? Will we strive prayerfully not to lose heart, but to be among those who preserve the seeds of faith on earth?

No counseling is of any value unless it is embraced in an accepting, positive response.

There is mystery, of course, in the presence of evil in the world. But there is no mystery concerning the stance God wants us to take and maintain with respect to it.

If ever we are tempted to think God is unconcerned about the evil, or that he is not supportive of us in our resistance to it, we will do well to think carefully about how we expect him to work his will in the world. His schedule and perspective may be quite different from ours. Dr. Leslie Weatherhead has made the helpful suggestion that God's will must be understood as three-dimensional. First, there is God's intentional will; then there is God's permissive will; and finally, there is God's ultimate will, what he keeps moving persistently toward despite all impediments.

Obviously, we do not understand all that is in the mind and heart of God. We only know that he is love, that his loving purpose is to redeem his lost people in their troubled world, and that by his grace we are invited into partnership with him in pursuit of this purpose.

If we are tempted to impatience in the process of achievement, let us rest assured that there is purpose in his patience. Let us trust him and not lose hope.

Ours is a religion of hope, you know. Unlike the pessimism in other great religions, the message in the Christian Gospel is a positive one, affirming life, the world, and the goodness of God. This is why Christians have the reputation of being incurable optimists.

For all of us who walk the tightrope of faith between hope and discouragement, James Weldon Johnson, the eminent black scholar, has provided a useful prayer formula. It is found in the Introduction to his little volume of Negro sermon poems entitled *God's Trombones*. A black layman is praying for the preacher before the sermon begins. He petitions God to put the preacher's eye "to the telescope of eternity" and let him "look upon the paper walls of time."

This, I am sure we can all agree, is what we need in the darkest moments of our struggle against evil. We need God's help in looking beyond the paper walls of time with eyes glued to the telescope of eternity.

Then perhaps we can understand, as Habakkuk came to understand, that "the vision awaits its time," and that the righteous must live by faith.

Zephaniah 3:1-9
Luke 18:9-14

Proper 25 (C)
Pentecost 23 (L)
Ordinary Time 30 (RC)

Let God Be God

The concern of the prophet Zephaniah, from whom one of the lessons was read this morning, was with a society of people who had drifted into a condition of moral and religious chaos. On the one hand, they were pretending to worship both Baal and the Lord. On the other hand, they were in reality a rebellious, defiled, and oppressive people who listened to no voice and accepted no correction from any source.

What Zephaniah saw as essential for them to do was to get their act together by learning to "call on the name of the Lord and serve him with one accord."

Jesus' parable in the lesson read from Luke's record of the Gospel deals with the problem of self-righteousness. Jesus saw a fundamental difference in the way a Pharisee and a tax collector prayed.

The focus in both these lessons, as you can see, is on the God problem. Who or what is being worshiped?

They point up the sad consequences of displacing allegiance to the living Lord, the one true God, with idolatry and anomie: idolatry being either of inanimate objects or exalted self, and anomie being undisciplined normlessness.

Now, have we any need to give special attention to these lessons? Are we having any difficulty deciding what to worship, or whether to worship anything? Is there any moral disorientation among us because we recognize no central source of authority and have no fixed point of reference by which to guide our behavior? Or have we, perchance, simply lost interest in the whole God concept? Should we be counted among those who seem to care not whether God is alive or dead?

This last question may be the most relevant of all. A lot of people today seem to look upon the God question as a dead issue. They may still give casual assent to the concept as an interesting mental artifact brought over from the past, but see little utility in it for their own living.

The stance of such persons is, at best, much like that of the little girl who wanted to know where God was. When told that God was everywhere she wanted to know if he was in the house, in her bedroom, behind the dresser, even under the bed on which she was being put to sleep. After having been assured that God was in all those places, she was later overheard saying an interesting and very candid prayer. "God," she was saying, "I know you are everywhere. I know you are in the house. I know you are in this room. I know you are behind that dresser and under this bed. But, God, if you move you'll scare me to death."

If we are willing to deal seriously with the issues raised by these Scriptures, there are several important points to be considered.

First, the need of a God in our lives must be recognized.

Even the most ancient ancestors of whom we have any record felt this need in a compulsive way. They turned in almost every direction they could think of in the quest for a spiritual reality to help them make sense of their lives. That quest, continued through the ages, evolved great religious traditions out of which have come some of our oldest, strongest, and most stable institutions.

Why have we humans had this need? We are flesh like other flesh, but this is a need that seems unique in the animal kingdom. It is a gift of grace. So far as we can tell, no other beings possess it. But what is it? What makes humans unable to live satisfying lives, as other beings appear to do, without being disturbed by a sense of need to be related to something other than and beyond themselves?

A possible cue to this mystery is found in the Genesis record of the capabilities and responsibilities given the first humans. God made Adam and Eve capable of naming the other beings found in the Garden of Eden, of discerning good from evil, and of answering the question of "Why?" when he thundered at them concerning their misdeeds. And he immediately began holding them responsible for the use of these capabilities.

Assess these unique human capacities carefully and you will see that we are not limited to what is concrete and adherent, to what we can see, hear, smell, feel, and taste. We can go beyond the physical senses to visualize the unseen, to ask questions, to seek answers, and to pursue meanings.

When humans name things they are ascribing values, which means that they have been seeking meanings in what they see. They do the same thing, also, when they try to understand what happens to them in their life experiences. In pursuit of the logic, the why of life, they have been drawn inexorably toward an understanding of God, the unseen source that lies back of and makes sense of all perceived reality.

As Augustine observed, their souls are restless until they find rest in God.

Humans are, then, spiritualizing beings. They look for essences in what they experience and perceive, and invent symbols to represent these essences. It was inevitable, therefore, that they would come to an understanding of the great, all-embracing spirit in whom rested the coherence and logic that made all other reality make sense.

The grand summary of this climactic development is found in the first verse of the Gospel according to John. "In the beginning," he says, "was the Word (*logos* in the Greek, or *logic* in the English derivative), and the Word was with God, and the Word was God."

It must be noted, however, that humans have sometimes become impatient with the spiritualizing process because they have found it trying and difficult. The physical side of their nature has demanded concreteness. Building an idol has been more satisfying than trying to understand and commune with the great Spirit whose face is not visible. Consequently, many a golden calf has been molded in preference to wrestling on mountain tops with the awesomely mysterious Yahweh.

Even where the use of concrete idols has been avoided, carelessness in the valuing and symbolizing process has resulted in spiritualized forms of idolatry. In such things as pride, prejudice, pursuit of pleasure or fame, grasp for power, and misplaced love, value perversions and distortions have occurred which have diverted attention from the true and living God without whom life's meanings fall apart.

Truly, there is only one real God, and without him we humans are lost. In the long course of human history he has made himself known in many ways. We know no better way of referring to him than to call him our loving heavenly Father.

This brings us to the second point of challenge in today's Scripture lessons, which is that we personally take stock of our spiritual condition. Are we involved in any idolatries that are interfering with our relationship to the true God so beautifully revealed in Jesus?

Let us not kid ourselves. It has been said that one's god is that to which he or she gives supreme allegiance. If that is so, the practice of idolatry is surely rampant in our midst. Our idols appear in many guises, and their shrines dot the landscapes of both private and public devotion. If we do not stay on guard alertly, we will be seduced into their worship without realizing what we are doing.

Are you and I willing to consider seriously the possibility that we are involved in some form of idolatry? Or that we are being tempted to become involved? What about the idolatrous self-centeredness that finds expression in greed, selfishness, arrogance, self-righteous pride, and possessive love? What about the worship of money, things, job, popularity, fame, power, or other benefits that can be gleaned from the life of community? Has business, racism, nationalism, class consciousness, sex, or other kinds of social or sensory experience become a religion with us?

These are only a few of the forms with which the Holy of Holies of our lives may be desecrated. Regardless of whether we make them exclusive occupants of that sacred place, or merely ask God to share it with them, we put our souls in jeopardy.

As many of the Old Testament writers were keenly aware, God is a jealous God. He does not take kindly to the idea of being asked to fit into a pantheon of deities. We cannot expect to find the blessings of peace, happiness, and fulfillment that God wants us to have so long as we deny him full sovereignty in our lives.

In his description of the Pharisee and the other sinner at prayer, Jesus indicated that the sovereignty issue had special reference to the contest between worship of self and worship of God. At another time, you will remember, when asked which was the greatest commandment, he had specified that love of self was legitimate, but only when subordinated to the love of God and equalized with love of neighbor. The self-righteousness of the Pharisee was a gross violation of this spirit so strongly emphasized by the law and the prophets.

We who think of ourselves as the good church people of our community should take heed. It was annoyance with people who "trusted in themselves that they were righteous, and despised others" that prompted Jesus to tell the story of the parable.

Note the condition of these people. They were alienated from God. Though they paid lip service to him, they had no sense of need of his grace. They figured they were saving themselves by means of their piety and good works. In defense of this exalted view of themselves, moreover, they had become alienated from their fellow human beings. Despising others put props under the feeling of being elevated above them.

This is the kind of tragedy that always accompanies self-idolatry. It shuts persons off from the love and grace of God depriving them of both the blessing and the privilege of serving as channels of this love and grace. God is dethroned; the self is deceived with a false sense of adequacy; the communion that gives strength and stability to community life is destroyed.

Shall we do a little probing close to home? What about the class consciousness that undergirds our private schools; builds housing ghettos for the privileged with walls around them and guards at the gate; arranges our churches to conform to social class divisions? What about the alienation and exploitation that occur in our economic arenas where greed excuses its depradations with intimations of inherent superiority?

These are but a few of the social patterns that egoistic pride and self-righteousness have structured in our midst. One need not be a Sherlock Holmes to find a host of others.

Several studies have shown, for instance, that persons who identify themselves as Christians and church members are more harshly judgmental and punitive in their attitudes toward social offenders than are persons who make no claims to such identity. The parallel to Jesus' description of the self-righteous Pharisee is so close as to be truly shocking. We should be grateful to Harvard's Professor Gordon Allport, however, for having done a study that shows that the Christians and church members who have seriously internalized the faith are more inclined to be compassionate and non-punitive in their attitudes than are persons who do not claim to be Christians or church members.

Are we being too complacent about conditions our sociologists have been pointing out: the greedy competition that is producing increasingly great social and economic inequities; the burgeoning of class consciousness and hardening of social class lines; the humiliating and punitive treatment of the poor and unsuccessful by our welfare system?

If Zephaniah were among us, what do you think he would

say? Would he find basis for a conviction that we, too, are in danger of becoming a community ravaged by roaring lions and ravenous wolves?

Let us not try to deny, then, that we have our problems with idolatry. Like all peoples in all times, we struggle with temptations to worship false gods.

Clearly, we are affected as a society, and must learn to deal with the problem at the level of our life together in community.

I am reminded of a question T. S. Eliot raises in one of his best known poems. "What is the meaning of this city?" he asks, seeking to discover whether the people merely dwell together to make money off of each other or are a true community.

This is a question with which every resident of every city, town, and hamlet should be challenged. The choice is before us. Either we will make our communities jungles of alienation and brutish competition, devoted to the worship of self-interest and a pantheon of related idols, or places of communion with one another that reflects our communion with the living, loving God.

In the final analysis, however, it is at the personal level that each of us has to deal most directly with the lure of false gods. To myself as surely as to you I must address the question: Who, where, or what is your God? In what direction are you investing the energy and passion of your life? By what value standards, from what source, are you being governed? Are you giving your whole life to the highest and best, or are you suffering the crippling of compromise between unsettled commitments?

Is it not time for us to make sure we are willing to let God be God in our lives? Will we be among those who have no other gods before him?

Are we willing to take a personal inventory by the standards of Zephaniah's concern? If so, we will be having to take an honest look at things that may be keeping us from calling on the Lord and serving him with gladness. Even if we are not bowing down to idols while pretending to serve the Lord, could it be that we are leaning toward the crowd of the rebellious and defiled who listen to no voice, accept no correction, and know no shame?

Shall we get serious about the possibility that Jesus' parable about the Pharisee and the tax collector may be applicable to us? Can we consider the possibility that we are contaminated with self-righteousness?

Are we comfortably proud of our goodness this morning? Are we so absorbed in self-interest that we are neglecting communion with God? Are we becoming so callous toward other people that we feel superior to them and indifferent to their needs? Or are our hearts filled with compassion and true empathy rooted in obedience to the love of God?

There is only one cure for the idolatry that shows itself in self-righteousness. That cure is in the humility that confesses sin and weakness and recognizes that we all are sinners saved only by God's grace. This is the only basis for dealing honestly with one's self, with God, and with neighbors in community. It is the way of salvation, without which any life is sure to be lost.

How great is our determination to let God be God? Shall we look back with understanding to the ancient one who was troubled by the idolatries around him, and resonate with him in declaring, with all the passion of our hearts, "As for me and my house, we will serve the Lord"?

Daniel 7:1-3, 15-18
Luke 6:20-36

All Saints' Sunday (C, L)
Ordinary Time 31 (RC)

Why Aspire to Sainthood?

Today on the church calendar is designated All Saints' Sunday. It is a time for remembering persons who through the generations have been so outstanding in faith and ministry that their lives have been a special blessing to all who have known them. As someone has said, they have adorned the Gospel of Jesus Christ, though it might be better to say they received the Gospel so fully that it adorned and glorified them.

Who are the saints? How many can you name? Saint Peter? Saint Stephen? Saints Matthew, Mark, Luke, and John? Saint Paul? Saint Barnabas — one of my favorites because his name, meaning Son of Encouragement, so appropriately describes him? Saint Francis of Assisi? Saint Augustine?

The Roman Catholic Church has a long list of those who have been canonized — usually some two hundred years after their deaths, and after a careful scrutiny of their lives, work, and continuing influence.

But have you ever known a saint personally? Of all the people with whom you are acquainted, are there any you consider to be saints?

Most of us probably would be hesitant to say that any particular individual we know actually is a saint. Yet each of us, no doubt, has someone in mind who is being thought of as a saintly person. Is it a parent, a grandparent, an uncle, an aunt, a teacher, a pastor, a doctor, a neighbor, a friend?

Of course, we do not see these persons as perfect. We have

no set of tedious criteria with which to measure them. No church bureaucracy has considered them for canonization. Yet we have witnessed a quality of faith and goodness in them that has inspired and blessed us. We thank God for them; we canonize them in our hearts.

As a congregation of people, let us be remembering with special gratitude this morning the many individuals who have made outstanding contributions to the rich heritage we enjoy in this place. How many there have been whose devotion to their Lord has found sacrificial expression in the building and maintenance of this church and its program! Their faithfulness in service, sacrificial giving, and loving devotion have had a formative influence on our lives and have provided us with open channels of opportunity for service. We bless them for all they have done, and trust that we can build on their example to expand the strength of this Body of Christ in our community.

It is, of course, highly appropriate that we should pay homage to the great souls of the past who have clearly reflected the revelation in Jesus. They have shown us how sincere faith in this revelation enables the image of God to show through our animal natures. We look upon them and are doubly assured that we are, as Jesus said, children of God, not mere *homo saps*.

This points up the fact, however, that we too should be candidates for sainthood. It is an option for us as surely as it has been for persons in the past. Are we taking the option seriously? Shall I ask each of us personally: Do *you* want to be a saint? If not, why not?

Some of us may be deflected from such an ambition by the notion that a saint has to be perfect and surrounded by a certain aura of ghostly supernaturalism. If so, we should be reminded that Jesus said no human being is perfect, and we should remember that his obvious concern was for the fulfillment of the highest potentials in the natural dimensions of our being. God does not want us to be ghosts or angels. He wants us to be the filled out, complete beings he had in mind when he gave us life. This, it seems to me, is the clearest intent in the salvation offered by Jesus.

It cannot be honestly said of any of the saints of whose lives we have detailed records, that they were perfect people. Look at the wobbly, vascillating, prejudiced Simon Peter! Consider Paul's hang-ups about women and sex! Remember the scars licentiousness left on Saint Augustine!

These and the many others were only human beings like you and me. Only in the depth and fulness of their response to God's call in Christ were they any different.

It will be a tragic mistake if we reject the goal of sainthood because the standard is so high. If we aim not at life's highest goal, to what level will we aspire?

If we listen carefully to what Jesus said in the lesson read this morning, we will be forced to acknowledge that the standards are exactingly high. He spoke of triumphal endurance in poverty, sorrow, and persecution; of compassionate sharing with persons less fortunate; of forgiving, loving, praying for, and turning the other cheek to enemies; of showing mercy and charity in all human relations; and of living, in summary, by a rule, appropriately called golden, of doing to others as you wish them to do to you.

But it must be remembered that Jesus was not a rigid, judgmental dogmatist. He was not laying down a law so much as he was pointing the way to authentic living. His words were not the imperious proclamations of an authoritarian ruler or judge, but the warm-hearted counsel and injunction of a concerned teacher and friend.

As a sociologist would say, he outlined an ideal typology toward which he enjoined his followers to strive. That any one of them, much less all of them, would perfectly embrace the ideal was neither expected nor implied.

Sadly, a lot of Jesus' would-be followers have stumbled in discouragement at this important point. Because they have concluded that the standards are too high to be reachable, they have given up on pursuit of them.

This has given rise to one of the interesting psychoanalytic theories attempting to account for the prejudice of anti-semitism. Christians, according to the theory, are basically deeply resentful of Jesus for imposing on them standards so unrealistically high as to seem practically unattainable. They cannot admit, however, that they resent, possibly even hate, Jesus for this.

Instead, they seek an outlet for their hostility in some other direction. Since Jews were associated with Jesus and involved in his crucifixion, and have also been competitively present with Christians in community life, they have served as a convenient scapegoat. On them the hostility can be more safely released.

Whatever one thinks of this theory, it is clearly indicative of an unfortunate misconception concerning the spirit in which Jesus set forth the high ideals for Christian living.

Does this kind of misconception account for the fact that we hesitate to say we are trying to be saints, or that we know other people who are saints? Can we identify sainthood in the making, in dynamic process, short of static perfection?

Perfectionism is a very different thing when viewed in dynamic rather than static terms. I shall be very disconcerted if after this service you confide in me that you are a saint, for I shall doubt that you have arrived at this level of perfection. If, however, you should tell me that you are earnestly striving to live a saintly Christian life, and praying to God to help you do so, I will rejoice and celebrate the commitment with you. While I doubt that you ever will be a perfect saint, I am confident that by God's grace and with his help you can be a "becoming saint."

What we are all concerned about, of course, is how the ideals set forth by Jesus get translated into the behavior of everyday living. What do persons look like who are in process of living saintly lives?

Some of you may remember an Italian-made film circulated

a number of years ago, entitled *Rocco and Brothers*. Despite the fact that English was dubbed in, it was a gripping movie. Rocco, sensitive, thoughtful, morally disciplined, and somewhat timid, was scorned and ruthlessly mistreated by his calloused, undisciplined oldest brother. Eventually, even, the only girl he ever loved was raped and murdered by this domineering sibling. Nevertheless, after learning that the murderer had been hiding behind a chimney on a rooftop for days without food or water, Rocco went to him in a spirit of compassion carrying food and drink. Upon hearing of it, one of the younger brothers exclaimed, "Rocco is a saint!"

There is a story also that comes to us from an earlier time in a remote peasant village of Europe. It tells of two neighbors. One was a churlish, unneighborly, evil man who kept a large, viscious dog with which he intimidated everyone who came near. The other was a good man who lived nearby with his wife and small son. All his overtures toward friendliness with his unpleasant neighbor were harshly rebuffed. Especially resented were his attempts to suggest that the dog be some way curbed or restrained.

Then one day the dog came into his yard, attacked the small son and killed him.

All the emotions of grief and hatred flooded the man's soul. He was inconsolable. The many painful, immobilized days and sleepless nights stretched into weeks and months as he pondered possibilities for revenge.

In the meantime, all the people of the village turned against the ugly neighbor. He was completely ostracized. No one would trade with him or sell him anything. Because he could not obtain seed, his field was fallow, and the prospect of starvation loomed ahead.

Finally, the grieving father began to experience a measure of victory and inner peace. In the middle of a night, his wife awoke to find him missing from their bedroom. Looking out a window, she saw him in the bright moonlight sowing the evil neighbor's field with his own seed.

Clearly, God can give people strength to overcome their baser impulses, to transcend the ordinary and commonplace in their human nature. He can endow them with power to live in terms of the highest they know.

It *is* possible to forgive one's enemies. It *is* possible to love people who are unlovely. It *is* possible to cultivate sensitivity of mind and heart, and to live in responsive, empathetic communion with other persons. A selfish life can be turned into a self-emptying one. A timid, cowardly life can become confident, courageous, and strong.

The grace of God makes it possible. It comes about through faith in Jesus Christ and commitment to the love of God revealed in him. And these, unquestionably, are points at which marks of sainthood begin becoming visible.

We must not be under any illusions, however. While such lifestyles are possible, they are not free or easy. Prayer, discipline, hard work, suffering, self-sacrifice, persistence, and even humiliation are commonplace involvements. Achievement and maintenance carry a price tag of eternal vigilance and personal anguish.

Consider Jesus, often at prayer, even sweating blood in Gethsemane, and finding strength on the cross to pray for his executioners. Consider Saint Paul, wrenching himself away from the church of his childhood, enduring harsh criticism, suffering imprisonment, having to make tents for a living, and pushing himself to his limits to spread the Gospel despite the burden of physical affliction. Remember Francis of Assisi, who turned away from a life of wealth and luxury. Suffer with Mother Theresa as she immerses herself in the misery of Calcutta's slums. And do not overlook the devout mothers and fathers who pour their whole lives into unselfish love for their children, the faithful church members who carry the burden of responsibility for maintaining the Body of Christ, the dedicated teachers and other community servants who live beyond the call of duty and the lure of copious paychecks with compassionate concern for others.

Yes, the price is high. The saints often find themselves "singing in the rain." Not uncommonly, in view of the odds they face, they experience such awe as that of the Breton fishermen in whose famous prayer is the exclamation, "O God, thy sea is so great, and our boats are so small!"

The price is high, but it is worth it. The rewards are nothing short of glorious.

Daniel, in the Word read today, assures us that "the saints of the Most High shall receive the kingdom, and possess the kingdom for ever, for ever and ever." In other words, they come into possession of the greatest meaning that life can hold, the supreme value in all creation. Nothing else in the universe compares with it. Eternity is in it, and it is eternally theirs.

In much the same vein, Jesus said if you love your enemies and do good "your reward will be great, and you will be sons of the Most High." That's what saints-in-the-making are, persons who are recognized by themselves and others as God's children.

It will be remembered also that Jesus on another occasion made the provocative statement that the Kingdom of God is "at hand" and "within you." Can we doubt that the message intended by this statement was that the Kingdom is inside us, in our midst, and within our reach? We can experience the Kingdom as individuals and communities of persons when God is given the opportunity to occupy the throne in our hearts.

The good news in the Gospel is our invitation to experience life in its fullest, most meaningful dimensions. It is an invitation to live victoriously in the confidence of unshakable security and belongingness. As theologian Paul Tillich might have put it, it is a challenge to root our existence in "the ground of our being."

What can be greater than for one to be known as a true child of God, unless it be the humble inner assurance that it is so? What greater wealth can enrich a life than that which is found in possessing the Kingdom of God?

Let us, then, resolve to take the high road with our lives,

the saintly road. Let us dare lay claim to our heritage as God's children. Let us not be afraid or ashamed to join Abraham and all the saints of all the ages in launching out toward the land God has promised we can possess.

The way will not be a lonely one. Our Lord has promised to accompany us on every step of it. He will give us victory over every painful encounter, and songs of rejoicing will fill our hearts.

Zechariah 7:1-10
Luke 20:27-38

Proper 27 (C)
Pentecost 25 (L)
Ordinary Time 32 (RC)

The Now-ness of Eternity

Can any of you tell me what time it is? It's all right to look at your watches now. (Just don't start looking at them and shaking them when I get into the middle of this sermon!)

How do you know what time it is, or what time *itself* is? There is a mystery in the concept of time that is difficult to comprehend. The one obvious fact about it is that it is related to perceptions of change. If there were no change, would the concept of time have any meaning?

Actually, we cannot answer such a question because change is the essence of our existence. Even the cells of our bodies are constantly changing and being replaced. We live in the cycles of night and day, the changing seasons, and the processes of aging.

Time and change are for us inseparably related. We cannot imagine a condition without either of them. We can only thank God for the fact that in the providence of creation the dimension of time was provided to accommodate change and make a place for us.

Yet the concepts of time and changelessness are all mixed up in our thinking about eternity and eternal life, which is what I want us to focus upon this morning. We fear and abhor death because it appears to be a condition both of absolute change and absolute changelessness. Our hearts are thrilled, therefore, with the Gospel's promise of eternal life. And we are like children thumbing our noses at the "grim reaper," as we join Paul in shouting, "O death, where is thy sting? O grave, where is thy victory?"

But how mature is our thinking about eternity and eternal life? Is our focus on changelessness, endless existence in time, endless change in an endless existence, or what? Is eternity out yonder, beyond this life, or does it embrace the here and now? Is eternal life quantitative or qualitative?

The point I wish to make, one that seems of paramount importance to me, is that we consider the *now-ness* of eternity and the qualitative character of eternal life.

In the lesson read this morning from the Gospel according to Luke, Jesus is quoted as saying to the Sadducees, who did not believe in the resurrection, that God is "not God of the dead, but of the living; for all live to him." That time had little bearing on the condition of eternal life he had already indicated. Those who are counted worthy of the resurrection from the dead, he had stated, do not engage in such change relationships as marriage, "for they cannot die anymore, because they are equal to angels and are sons of God."

In his follow-up response to a question from the Pharisees, who *did* believe in the resurrection, he made plain what he considered to be the essence of the kind of religion that put the quality of eternity into life. It was, he said, in the whole-hearted loving of God and neighbor.

I freely admit that I may be as confused as the next person about eternity and the nature of eternal life. The limitations in my understanding are highly visible to me. I am still struggling, for example, with the words of the old Sunday church school song that spoke of "when the trumpet of the Lord shall sound and time shall be no more." I am plagued with visions of life after death being related to gates of pearl, streets of gold, white robes, happy singing, and endlessly monotonous pleasant existence.

I can't avoid sentiments similar to those of Charles G. Blanden, who wrote a little poem in which he said:

> *I cannot think of Paradise a place*
> *Where men go idly to and fro,*
> *With harps of gold and robes that shame the snow;*
> *With great wide wings that brightly interlace*
> *Whenever they sing before the Master's face —*
> *Within a realm where neither pain nor woe,*
> *Nor care is found; where tempests never blow;*
> *Where souls with hopes and dreams may run no race.*
> *Such paradise were but a hell to me;*
> *Devoid of all progression, I should rot,*
> *Or shout for revolution, wide and far.*
> *Better some simple task, a spirit free*
> *To act along the line of self forgot —*
> *Or help God make a blossom or a star.*

Charles G. Blanden, "Paradise," in *1000 Quotable Poems, An Anthology of Modern Verse*, compiled by Thomas Curtis Clark, Vol. I, (Chicago: Willett, Clark & Company, 1937), p. 334.

In my confusion, however, I have a growing conviction that eternity is now, and that eternal life is essentially a quality of existence. This may not be all, but it is for me the foundational concept. It is what comes through most vividly to me in the many words and images of the Scriptures.

A simplistic analogy was brought to my mind somewhere along the line in the days of my schooling. I am sure it is nothing new to most of you, but I have cherished it as both provocative and intriguing.

It states that if you and I could maintain sight of this scene in this moment in time and be swept away from it at the speed of light, we would see it as forever remaining the same, unchanging. As I ponder this, I find myself thinking that God is unfettered by time and space and has the perspective of infinity. In his sight, therefore, every moment and movement of our existence must be fixed in his awareness. It is all a part of eternity.

Was it in this sense that Jesus said God "is not God of the dead, but of the living; for all live to him"? In other words, are all who have ever lived always alive to God in all the terms and conditions of their existence?

Whatever the answer may be to such intriguing questions, one fact is crystal clear. A yearning for eternal life is structured in the makeup of the human heart and mind. More than this, eternity, like a magnet, exerts a constant tug on our daily living. It prompts us through conscience to distinguish between right and wrong, and to choose the right. It stirs in us the ethicizing impulse to grope beyond what *is* toward that which *ought to be*. And by thus involving us in the valuing process it draws us toward the kind of living that has enduring quality in it.

It was the tug of eternity that prompted the prophet Micah to ask, "What doth the Lord require of thee?" And it was a magnificent insight into truth that enabled him to see the answer: life with God, life with eternity in it, is in doing justly, loving kindness, and walking humbly with God. (Micah 6:8)

The poet Joseph Addison, in trying to account for our longing for immortality, concluded that

'Tis the divinity that stirs within us,
'Tis heaven itself that points out an hereafter
And intimates eternity to man.

Joseph Addison, "Immortality," from "Cato," as quoted in *1000 Quotable Poems, An Anthology of Modern Verse,* compiled by Thomas Curtis Clark, Vol. I, *Ibid.,* p. 324.

There should be no doubt about it. God wants us to live, to have life and have it abundantly. He proved it in the sacrifice Jesus made for our salvation — salvation that meant fulfillment, the filling out in our lives of the dreams God had for us. In Jesus he put squarely and clearly before us the way to eternal life, the kind of life that endures forever.

Eternal life, therefore, is not merely a concern of ours. It is God's concern for us. What we long for God is working for — and seeking our cooperation in the process.

As the Scriptures remind us, however, eternal life is God's

gift to us, a pure act of his grace. We cannot produce it or earn it. We can only accept it or destroy our chances to enjoy it.

Though there was neither a rebuke nor a full explanation of the mysteries involved, Jesus' response to the Sadducees was clearly a challenge to take a fresh look at the whole question of eternal life. Can we sense the challenge to take a fresh look at our own thinking on the matter? To do so should help us toward a better stance for faith and living, even though the mystery may remain with many puzzling points to ponder.

Shall we consider, for example, that our longing for eternal life may be primarily an expression of our fear of death? If this is the case, shouldn't we be looking for a more positive basis? A negative attitude toward death seems a poor substitute for a positive attitude toward life. Moreover, important as it is, physical existence is not the only measure to be used for life. The testimony of martyrs through the ages has been that there are things more important to life than life itself.

We may well ask ourselves, too, how we see this life in relationship to the life we anticipate after physical death. Is it continuous or discontinuous? Do we see this present life as a testing, prelude, or qualifying run for the real life to come? Or are we looking upon our day-to-day existence here as an integral part of eternal experience? Seeing eternity as being now, versus viewing it as beginning after physical death, can make a great deal of difference in our living.

Very possibly, however, the most important consideration has to do with where we are in our thinking about eternal life in quantitative-versus-qualitative terms. Are we focused on it as an endless extension of time, or as a fellowship with God and all his saints in the appreciation and enjoyment of the highest values and meanings that life can give? After all, what meaning could endless existence in time have for persons who have never really lived — in the sense of entering with God into the fulfilling dimensions of life for which they were created?

Life that has never begun cannot be ended; nor can life

that has embraced enduring quality ever be denied the meaning of its reality.

Yes, my friends, life can be eternal. It is a gift of God's grace, guaranteed in Jesus' life and by his death on the cross. Eternal life is ours to appropriate and experience in the here-and-now, and for all of reality that stretches beyond the boundaries of time. Neither physical death nor the end of time can obliterate the meaning in it.

The keys to the Kingdom in which life of the eternal kind is experienced are found on many pages of the Scriptures. To Zechariah the Lord said, "Render true judgment, show kindness and mercy each to his brother, do not oppress the widow, the fatherless, the sojourner, or the poor; and let none of you devise evil against his brother in your heart."

Micah's words about justice, kindness, and humility, which we have already noted, are by no means unique. In one way or another they are echoed throughout the Bible.

In very concrete terms, Jesus spelled out the emphasis on loving God and neighbor. Judgment, he indicated, occurs where one's relationship is defined in response to persons experiencing such conditions as hunger, poverty, sickness, imprisonment, estrangement, or other forms of distress or need. In such human relations is revealed one's relationship to God, and all that is eternal hinges on that relationship.

In this light, Jesus' injunction to seek first "the Kingdom of God and his righteousness" takes on special meaning. This is the highway that leads to eternal life.

The bottom line for all of us in this consideration is whether we are willing to accept the gift of eternal life and begin the process of enjoyment, growth, and fulfillment that are the basic dividends of its reality.

The Apostle Paul obviously was very here and now conscious when he enjoined the Corinthians, saying: "Behold, now is the acceptable time; behold, now is the day of salvation." (2 Corinthians 6:2) Will you hear him, and begin *now* to live the life that is eternal?

Malachi 4:1-6
Luke 21:5-19

Proper 28 (C)
Pentecost 26 (L)
Ordinary Time 33 (RC)

Life in the Sunbelt

Remember the song: "That's what I like about the South"?

There appears to be something special about the southern area of our nation. People who live there seem to love it. They say its good for your health. Industry is shifting in that direction. Flocks of snowbirds flee there from winter's drabness in the North. People like me dream of someday owning a place in Florida.

The sunbelt draws us. There is promise in thoughts of it. It must have been a southerner who wrote the old song that says, "Cheer up, my brother, live in the sunshine."

In the Word we have read from Malachi we find an admonition that we live our lives in the sunlight of God's love, assured of his grace and mercy, and governed by his righteousness. The implication is that, even when the drabness of winter and a hostile climate surrounds us, we have the certain promise of sunshine ahead. Sunlight will brighten the lives of those who live with confidence in God's promise of life in the sunbelt.

The people to whom Malachi spoke had learned that life can be bruising and discouraging for persons who try to live by the rules of conscience and faith. They had been kicked around in the jungle of a society where brutishness and selfishness seemed to reign supreme. Because of their sensitivities and value restraints they had been exposed, unprotected, and defined as weaklings in their own eyes as well as in the eyes of others.

Like salt rubbed in the wound of their suffering and humiliation, moreover, was their observation of other persons who seemed to live without conscience or regard for God's will, and who seemed to get by with it in jolly good fashion. Not surprisingly, these troubled ones were being tempted to conclude that their faith and disciplined way of life were not worthwhile.

"It is vain to serve God," they were saying. "What is the good of our keeping his charge or of walking as in mourning before the Lord of hosts? Henceforth we deem the arrogant blessed; evil doers not only prosper but when they put God to the test they escape."

To the darkness of this mood the Lord spoke through his prophet saying, in essence, "Hang in there, stay faithful to the law of Moses, and don't give in to your discouragement." There was nothing solid or of enduring value, the prophet assured them, in the lives of the arrogant and evildoers. Time would tell. Judgment was in the order of creation. The day would come, "burning like an oven," when all these evil ones would be consumed like stubble, leaving them "neither root nor branch."

"But for you who fear my name," said the Lord, "the sun of righteousness shall rise, with healing in its wings. You shall go forth leaping like calves from the stall."

What vivid and delightful imagery!

This theme of the ultimate triumph of faith and righteousness is sounded again and again throughout the Bible. There is a wide, wide sunbelt in the plans of God's mercy. His people must never forget the promise of it. Indeed, to remember it is to live always in the sunshine.

Jesus, in the lesson read from Luke's record of the Gospel, keeps matters even more clearly in the context of present, ongoing experience. He speaks of dark days of social turmoil, natural disasters, and personal suffering. His followers may expect great hardship and persecution. The faithful, however, must let the sunshine radiate through their lives. In full confidence that they are in God's loving care, they must look upon all such trying circumstances as opportunities to bear witness. By virtue of faithful endurance, moreover, they will gain their lives, or come into full possession of their souls.

Clearly, Jesus is calling upon his followers to be realistic about life. In a sense he is instructing them as to what life is all about. They are to expect trials and tribulations, but they must live responsibly in the midst of them, testifying always to their confidence in God and his love. And through that testimony the light in their lives will shed light in the world.

Do these two selections from the Scriptures speak to our condition? Do we find life hard and often discouraging? Are we sometimes tempted to feel that it is not worthwhile to try to live morally disciplined and compassionately caring lives? If so, these messages surely are for us. They urge us to look beyond the darkness to the sunbelt — indeed, to tap the sunshine in God's love and funnel it into the darkness around us.

In another instance, it will be remembered, Jesus specifically told his followers that they were the light of the world. Thus he implied that the sunshine was in them and that they could take it wherever they went. Can we doubt that this is our calling: to live in the sunshine ourselves, and help spread light in the world's darkness?

Remember the old saying that all the darkness in the world cannot smother out the light of one tiny candle?

How are we witnessing in this dark age of nuclear madness? What light are we shedding in the jungles of racial and religious bigotry? Where is our influence in the bloody arena of economic greed and social injustice?

Truly, the world in which we live is full of darkness. Are we cowering in its deepest recesses, afraid to uncover the light of our faith? Are we so intimidated, for example, that we dare not speak out against the manufacture and threatened use of nuclear weapons? Against arrogant nationalism? Against religious bigotry? Against racial prejudice and discrimination? Against the ruthless greed that fattens the rich and oppresses the poor? Are not such as these among the monstrous shadows that hover over us?

How shall humanity be led from under these shadows if we fail in our Christian responsibility? Are we not commissioned to witness to the love of God revealed in Jesus? Where is there hope for a world plunging ever into deeper darkness if this witness is not given with enthusiasm and effectiveness?

Who can doubt that a significant difference would be made if each of us, in fully determined commitment, should resolve, in the words of the children's song, that "This little light of mine, I'm gonna let it shine, let it shine, let it shine"?

Some of the brightest pages in human history tell of the examples of persons who lived their lives in the sunshine and carried the light with them into some of the world's dreariest corners of darkness. Many of us have heard of Father Damien, who went to the lepers' island to give hope to the hopeless, and of Mother Theresa who has brightened the squalor of India's worst slums. We have witnessed the martyrdom of Martin Luther King, Jr., who marched steadfastly into the darkness of America's racial bigotry and injustice with the shining light of Christian faith on his countenance.

Some of us have read Billy Graham's story (*Reader's Digest,* September, 1986) of Rachel, sister of Nate Saint, whom Graham had known in college. Nate and four other young missionaries were murdered in the Ecuadoran jungle while trying to take the Gospel to the fierce Auca tribe. When Rachel heard of her brother's death, she determined that she would reach the Aucas and translate the Scriptures into their language. With great courage, she finally contacted the tribe, and won acceptance among them. Living under primitive conditions in one of their huts, she achieved the translation and also shared the Good News through personal testimony. Among her first converts was Kimo, one of her brother's killers. Eventually he was brought to America, where he showed the blowgun and poison darts he had used, but testified that he no longer used them for such purposes because he now had the love of God in his life.

Countless are the unsung Christian heroes and heroines, however, of whom no record this side of heaven has been written, who have lived in the light of faith and transformed darkness into light. I am thinking of mothers and fathers who struggled against dreary odds to give their children decent homes and the blessing of faith and love; of business men and women who maintained ethical standards even when it meant personal loss; physically afflicted and permanently disabled persons who have manifested a triumphant spirit; frustrated and disappointed persons whose faith has kept them from giving in to despair. How much longer the list could be made! In the sunlight of God's love they constitute an endless line of splendor.

A point to remember, my friends, is that Jesus did not promise us a rose garden, a beautiful, easy, or painless existence. Ours is not an escapist religion, but a triumphant one. What Jesus did promise us was abundantly meaningful lives.

The pathway of our lives leads us inevitably into many dark and shadowy places. Some measure of frustration, pain, suffering, disappointment, envy, fear, temptation, or sorrow is sure to befall us. And over the pathway of every life hangs the shadow of our eventual physical demise.

The question is not whether we will experience the darkness, but how we will conduct ourselves in it — what kind of light will be lit for us as we go through it. The experience can make us weak and anemic. If the darkness penetrates our souls, it can destroy us. Let us thank God, however, that, no matter how dark the pit of depression into which we fall, faith can open the windows of heaven and let the sun of righteousness shine in.

Well remembered is the friend dying with cancer who, with lighted countenance, spoke of the experience as an opportunity to witness to his faith in Christ and the hope of eternal life.

Tolstoy, the noted author, told a depressing story for which he could see no happy ending. A footsore traveler, according to the story, was crossing a treeless plain when a ferocious beast began pursuing him. When an old abandoned well appeared in his path, the man leapt into it without giving the matter a second thought. As he plunged over the curb, however, he caught sight of a huge, open-jawed monster waiting for him at the well's bottom. Naturally, he began grabbing frantically for anything that might help break his fall. About halfway down, he managed to grasp a small thorny bush that was growing between the rocks with which the well was lined.

There the poor man hung: his hands torn and bleeding from the thorns; the beast above roaring and trying to reach down to him; the monster below hungrily awaiting him. To add to his agony, he saw two mice, a black one and a white one, come out from between the rocks and begin gnawing their way round and round the base of the little thorn bush to which he was clinging.

In total despair, the poor man closed his eyes at this point and began licking with his tongue at the tiny drops of nectar he had seen on the leaves of the thornbush.

This is the predicament in which Tolstoy left him.

The story was the author's way of saying that life is a dreadfully painful ordeal that can only end in the waiting jaws of death. The best one can do, therefore, is to resign oneself to it and take from it such small pleasures as are possible while it lasts.

What Tolstoy was unable to see was the possibility of a happier ending. The scenario might have said that the owner of the estate witnessed what was taking place, and sprang quickly into action. Grabbing arms, he hastened to drive the beast away, after which he lowered a rope to the terrorized man and drew him to safety. It could have described how, after the rescue, the poor fellow was taken to the master's home, where his wounds were dressed, food and fresh clothing were given him, and he was invited to remain as long as he wished.

Such an ending would have been in far greater conformity with Christian faith.

God's challenging message to us, then, through Malachi and Jesus, is a double-barrelled one. It is a challenge to maintain faith and hope, no matter how trying or desperate the circumstances of our lives. But it is more. It is a challenge to put our faith to work positively and creatively, whatever the circumstances in which we may find ourselves. The trying time is the time of our opportunity to bear testimony.

A simple logic is found in the scriptural formula for God-blessed, triumphant living. It relates first to the fact that God is our father and we are his children, sharing in his creative nature. From this it follows that the purpose of our existence is to fellowship with God in the exercise of our creative endowment, functioning in faith as definers and valuers of all that life presents us. As we are faithful in the defining and valuing process, relating that which is finite to that which is eternal, we experience the fulfillment of our being. As Jesus said, we gain our lives.

We must not shrink from taking an honest look at the drab realities around us. The world of human society is indeed a dark and dreary place in our time: so much strife and greed; so much prejudice and alienation; so many inequities and injustices; so great a threat of nuclear destruction.

But let our Christian witness bring light into these dark corners of our common life. Let us look beyond them to the sunrise that can bring the healing power of God's love to bear upon the conditions that produce them.

Above all, let us not submit to personal discouragement or despair. To myself as surely as to you, let me say: No matter how trying or desperate the circumstances of your life may be, resolve to live by responsible faith in the sunlight of God's unfailing love. Open your heart and let God help you live so creatively and triumphantly that even "the valley of the shadow of death" will hold for you no terror.

And if perchance there is one among us groping in the deep, cold darkness of unconfessed and unrepented sin, let me urge you to take hold of Christ and let him lead you into the sunlight of God's forgiving love, where you may dwell in the sunbelt of new life and hope.

2 Samuel 5:1-5   Christ the King
John 12:9-19

The Reins of Power

In keeping with the directives of our church calendar, we celebrate Christ the King today.

As we do so, two great events are in the background of our thinking. One has to do with the occasion when the Israelites came to David at Hebron and petitioned him to take on the additional responsibility of being their king as well as the king of Judah. The other is the remembrance of Jesus riding a donkey into Jerusalem, and being acclaimed a king by the excited multitude that had gathered, because they had heard that he had raised a man from the dead.

David accepted the kingship, with the idea of being a shepherd king. And he did a reasonably good job of it for thirty-three years, although there were times when he let himself be corrupted by the power of his office.

Jesus, on the other hand, apparently never thought of himself as a king, and probably was uncomfortable with the appellation. He accepted the people's shallow adulation, but did not let it go to his head. His was much more truly the spirit of shepherd.

In both these instances is evidence of the fact that human beings individually and collectively feel weak and inadequate. They long for protective power, and seek it in power figures outside of and beyond themselves. That's why they invented kings in the first place, and why they persist in leaning on Jesus in infantile fashion.

There is every reason to believe that Jesus did not want his relationship to his followers to be that of a king to his subjects. The thrust of his Gospel was toward empowerment, not subjugation. He wanted God's children to recognize and use the power of God that was available to them by God's grace: power to grow up and achieve maturity; to live victoriously and redemptively; to take up crosses and overcome the world of temptation and evil.

Yes, we celebrate Christ the King today. But is it not with about the same amount of confusion in our minds as that which animated the crowd that waved palm branches and scattered them along the way from Bethany to Jerusalem so long ago?

There is incongruity here, even as there was on that day when Jesus took his famous donkey ride. What do we mean by acclaiming him in such terms as that of king? How many Americans are there who are willing to submit to the rule of a king of any kind?

And how fitting was it ever to speak of the humble Jesus as a king? We who are inclined to celebrate the fact that there are few lords and kings left in the world may do well to take heed to what we are saying. Is there in our proclamation the same element of insincerity and satire that was in the placard the Romans nailed to his cross, mocking him as the "King of the Jews"?

An interesting letter came to my attention recently. It was from a person caught up in the spirit of Women's Lib. The writer was questioning why we persist in imaging God as Father, and Jesus as Lord and King. To such questions I find no easy answer, except that the terms are used in the Bible and church tradition and come out of a distant past in which society was organized along patriarchal and authoritarian lines. The terms seemed most appropriate in the context of the times in which they were first used, and we have continued to use them out of respect for their traditional value. To many of us, however, they are now archaic and somewhat anachronistic. Certainly they reflect attitudes and arrangements of a society structured around male dominance.

The more one ponders the letter writer's questions, however, the more it becomes obvious that the real problem being wrestled with is not the matter of sexual identity in the imagery. It is the problem of power and its use.

In early patriarchal society the father had the power of a despot. Lords and kings were male power figures. It is the abuses of power associated with maleness through the ages and down to the present that bothers those who are identified with the Women's Liberation Movement. And while we do not need any more war between the sexes, it is obvious that these abuses need to be corrected.

Since, then, power is in large measure what is being connoted when we speak of Jesus as Lord and King, let us give consideration to power and how it relates to the reality in Jesus and in us.

It seems especially appropriate that we should do so. Dramatic developments in our time are making us increasingly aware that the whole universe is a vast dynamo of energy. The astounding amount of energy in an atom, we have discovered, is integral to that which keeps the stars in their courses, green in the grasses, current in our light globes, and life flowing through our veins. Energy is power, and the reality and awesome wonder of physical energy and power in this universe is the most impressive feature of our environment.

The amount of control God is granting us over matter and physical energy is, at one and the same time, amazing, gratifying, and frightening. The uses and abuses of physical power under human control constitute a challenge of unprecedented magnitude.

But physical power is not the only kind that flows in the universe. God the Creator, the all-powerful energizer, is a spirit, and his energy flows in spiritual as well as physical channels. Don't ask me to explain it. I can only report the reality.

I do not hesitate to express a conviction, however, that it is in the realm of the spirit that we are most in need of control.

Shall we turn to Jesus as an authoritarian ruler who will make us behave in the uses of this power, or punish us when we misbehave? Or shall we permit him to guide and teach us so that we may grow into the maturity and self-control God seeks in us?

Let's take a moment to ponder the nature of spiritual energy and power.

We know it in the experiences of love and prayer. We see a hint of it in various forms of social organization. When the role of kings was invented, as for example, at the time when Saul and David were crowned, group life took on a cohesiveness and strength that it had not had before. Individuals were not as sovereign as they were to become in a democracy, but separately and collectively they were stronger and more secure than they had been in tribal anarchy. Something intangible, an element of pride and morale, was added, along with increased physical power.

The same thing happens when eleven miscellaneous individuals are converted into a successful football team. Power is added that the eleven separated from one another do not possess.

Nations become great concentrations of physical power. The high morale of a strongly patriotic spirit, however, can spell the difference between effective national strength and debilitating weakness.

Even so, the best examples of spiritual power are found in the lives of persons, and in those human relationships where love or hate flows.

The power of redeeming love that flowed from Jesus on the cross is still sweeping the world. By contrast the hate the Nazis generated blighted and almost destroyed the world.

What a world of difference, too, a loving family makes in the development of personhood in a child! The matron of a detention center for juvenile delinquents underscored this when she reported her conviction that a delinquent girl in her charge had never known what it was to be loved.

What power on earth is more impressive than that which flows through such a life as that of a Saint Francis of Assisi, an Albert Schweitzer, or a Martin Luther? What comparable power could transform a drunkard like Sam Jones or an uneducated shoe store clerk like Dwight L. Moody into great Christian evangelists; or turn a young, black, Baptist preacher, like Martin Luther King, Jr., in Montgomery, Alabama, into a victor over deeply entrenched racial bigotry in our land? In Moses, too, its uniqueness is seen where it changed a stammering coward into an iron-willed oracle of God and leader of people.

Indeed, there is another realm of power that is related to and even more awesomely wonderful than, the realm of physical power. It is to this realm that Jesus seeks to help us become effectively related. Control in this realm is essential to meaningful control in the physical realm. Without it we will never be free of such horrors as slavery, Nazi madness, brutal South African coercion, violent crime, greedy exploitation, war, and the threat of nuclear holocaust.

But how shall the control be effected? Shall we spend our time and energy begging God and King Jesus to deliver it as a gift to us? Or is it possible that God was telling us through Jesus to pick up the reins of responsible management of the power he has entrusted to us?

Jesus made it plain that in the realm where the Spirit of God prevails there is power like that in a grain of mustard seed, or the yeast that leavens dough: power to move mountains, turn hate into love, overcome evil with good, free the human heart from the burden of sin, and put love of neighbor on a par with self-love. At the same time, too, he pointed out that, while we should make the desire for this realm the prayerful passion of our lives, we should recognize that it is within our reach and must be established within us. As surely as he invited us to take up our crosses and follow him, he was challenging us to pick up the reins of power and live responsible lives in keeping with the will of God.

We *can* live meaningful, fulfilled lives. We *can* conquer the passions of envy, hate, greed, and selfishness. We *can* do something about the terrible social problems that are devastating human society.

In a very basic sense the issues are up to us. God's power is available to us, but it must be tapped through faith.

Dr. Norman Vincent Peale, who has made such an impression with his emphasis on the power of positive thinking, has a favorite sermon entitled "Imprisoned Splendor." In it he stresses the importance of letting faith enable one to achieve God-given potentialities.

We are, to be sure, dependent on the power of God. But God is love, and God seeks only that we love him in return, live in harmony with his love, and be empowered by it.

The keys of faith that will unlock the doors of our lives to this empowering love have been placed in our hands. Jesus urges us to use them with courage and confidence.

Remember how Jesus prayed for the disciples in the Upper Room after his last supper with them? He did not ask God to take over their lives and rescue them from the evil world. Rather, he prayed for them that evil would not gain control of them. And in his concluding word, after the prayer, he admonished them to carry on with courage, knowing that he had not been defeated but that he had conquered the world.

If we really understand him, we will know that Jesus is our friend, not one who wants to take over and run our lives. The only power he seeks over us is the power of persuasive, redeeming love.

He wants to see us accept responsibility for our lives, exercise faith, and receive God's power, as he had received it, to live victoriously. The requirements, as the Apostle Paul put them in the Phillips translation of his letter to the Ephesians (5:1-15), are simply that we live our lives "in love . . . as children of the light . . . with a due sense of responsibility."

So why, then, do we live with so much defeat in our lives? Why do we struggle so hard to get control of such powers as money, prestige, education, success, which cannot assure us happiness and fulfillment, while neglecting to take the reins of power for victorious living that Jesus holds out to us?

Why should we live as carelessly as the young rural swains of a generation gone by who went courting and carousing in horse-drawn buggies? Shall we, like many of them, so exhaust ourselves that we cannot stay awake on the way home in the wee hours, drop the reins on the dashboard, and hope the nag we are driving will find the way with us to the destination we desire?

Life is too important for us to take that chance. Let us listen to Jesus, wake up, and live with clear-eyed purpose and assurance.

And if by chance we find ourselves in the crowd praising him as king without understanding his mission, let us be free to join in the chant, but with a perceptive difference. Let ours be an expression of joy in the knowledge that he is a shepherd king, a friend and helper, not an autocratic king. Let us, in the spirit of the song writer, proclaim, "The King of Love My Shepherd Is."

About the Author

Haskell Morris Miller grew up on a farm in Hill County, Texas. Having committed himself to the ministry while in high school, he was ordained at an early age in the Cumberland Presbyterian Church. He attended Bethel College in McKenzie, Tennessee, for three years before transferring to Southern Methodist University, where he was granted the B.A. and M.A. degrees. Subsequently, he received the Ph.D. in sociology at New York University.

Before transferring into The Methodist Church in 1944, he served Cumberland Presbyterian pastorates in Dallas, Texas, the East Texas oilfield, and Knoxville, Tennessee. In The Methodist Church (now the United Methodist Church), he served as pastor in Gate City, Virginia, as vice-president of Emory and Henry College, Emory, Virginia, as Chaplain and Head of the Sociology Department at the University of Chattanooga, and for twenty years as Professor of Sociology and Social Ethics at Wesley Theological Seminary in Washington, D.C.

His writings include a half dozen books and numerous articles in a variety of publications.

He is married to Ada Wilson Anderson, of Paris, Tennessee. They have three children and twelve grandchildren. Their retirement home is at Rehoboth Beach, Delaware.

www.ingramcontent.com/pod-product-compliance
Lightning Source LLC
Chambersburg PA
CBHW060852050426
42453CB00008B/947